15 Steps
To Becoming
A Successful
(Artist)
Screenwriter

By

Sterling Anderson
with
W. Douglas Baker, PHD

ISBN: 978-0-9861446-4-6

Dedication

A special thanks to Ann Anderson for that fateful day when you arrived at Emerson Junior High School to defend the honor of your two favorite boys, Norman and Doug, against allegations of mischievous behavior. This book is for you.

CONTENTS

Becoming A Writer:
"There Are No Shortcuts"

Afriend and student, Will, once asked me to show
him how to become an actor and work in
Hollywood. Since I knew him as a diligent martial
artist, and as the son of my master Tae Kwon Do
instructor, I agreed to let him stay with me as he learned
his way around Hollywood and the opportunities there for
aspiring actors. It soon became apparent that I could help
best by providing him with particular perspectives and
principles, ones based on my twenty-five years of
experiences as an actor and as a screenwriter. I composed
a list and presented him with fifteen steps that would
lead him towards accomplishing his dreams of becoming
an actor. However, I emphasized, "There are no shortcuts;
you have to do the work."

Two years later, as he was preparing for his first
major role in a feature film, he handed me the list, each
item checked, and smiled, "I completed them all." His
career launched and took him far beyond his original
expectations. The invitations for roles in movies, or
appearances on television, streamed in. Soon, after his
initial success, *People* magazine listed him as one of the
"50 Sexiest People in Hollywood," one more indicator that
Will's dedication to his craft and goals was paying off.

I cannot guarantee that you will travel along the
scintillating path that Will created with the help of the

fifteen steps. But, similar to Will, if you reflect on and incorporate the suggested practices into your daily regimen, you will discover what we have: consistent, systematic work and perspiration propel you towards achieving your goals as a writer, or other type of artist.

The focus of this short book is on principles and practices that underlie the artistic process, particularly for writers, and writing for television or film is the impetus for each step. However, aspiring actors, artists, and composers can similarly employ these principles and practices towards attaining their goals and dreams, as Will demonstrated. Read through the steps, reflect on each, and envision how you will turn the suggestions into action. And write!

You may already view yourself as a writer; however, knowing how to write and feeling comfortable in one particular genre of writing does not guarantee success in another. The "transference" of supposedly autonomous skills (i.e., skills that you can pack into a toolbox and employ during any writing situation or event) ignores the social context, or situated nature of writing, and misrepresents the transformational process required to learn how to successfully write for particular purposes and audiences (e.g., teleplays and screenplays—see Step Thirteen). However, building on your experiences and on what you know will enable you to explore, envision, and enact these steps towards achieving your goals as a screenwriter.

How to Read this Book:
Layers of Intersecting Actions

Although the suggested principles and practices are presented as steps, they are not linear. That is, completing the first step does not necessarily lead you to the second one; in fact, I could argue that the fifteenth step ("Be fearless") is a prerequisite for the others. Therefore, consider viewing the steps as layers of intersecting actions or ways of engaging in practices that will help you become a disciplined, prolific screenwriter.

Steps One – Five. The first five steps are intended to urge you to *own* your goal of writing screenplays and for you to initiate ways of working as a writer. To become a screenwriter, you must dare to take risks of turning your story—or those of others—into scripts that will be critiqued (sometimes viciously), ones that will potentially earn labels of "failure" or "success." Yet, it is through your audacity to write and submit your screenplays for critique that leads you towards meeting your goals.

Steps Six – Ten. In the next five steps, I describe ways to turn your goals into actions, particularly through learning about and emulating the practices of other writers who have come before you. Yes, writers strive to describe or show life in unique ways, but building on the work or ideas of others is part of the process.

...uncovering sustainable motivation
is one of the keys to... my work ethic...

Steps Eleven – Fifteen. For the concluding five steps, I turn inward and reveal perspectives that anchor my discipline and energy as a writer. These final suggestions may appear therapeutic, but I have learned the value of reflecting on my motivation to write. I have discovered that uncovering *sustainable motivation* (see Step Thirteen) is one of the keys to how I approach the necessary discipline of the cyclical process of writing a screenplay: envisioning a story or character, sitting down and typing first drafts, re-envisioning, rewriting, listening to criticism of others, and layering. This approach sustains my work ethic as I continue rewriting until I "get the words right," as Hemingway responded when asked why had he rewritten the ending to his novel *A Farewell to Arms* thirty-nine times.

Turning stories into screenplays is exhilarating, and if you're willing to engage in the practices of screenwriters and *do the work*, you can achieve your dreams of seeing your writing transformed into film. The journey begins by owning your goal and declaring, "I'm a writer!"

One final note before your journey begins. I recognize that you may have personal circumstances that you believe constrain what you can achieve, and I certainly respect that we all have different loads to carry. At times, I allude to suggestions of how to engage in a particular step for those of you with limited resources, including time. However, writing successfully demands commitment, even if you can only chip away at a script for ten minutes a day (see Step Three). Start writing your teleplay or screenplay today!

Step One:
Own it.

Own it. Say, "I'm a writer." You have to state that you are a writer and that you will make time to write each day. Own your ambition, play the role, and learn the practices of writers. Stand before others and say what you've chosen as your life's work. Other professionals flash business cards and *proclaim* their profession, recognizing the value of marketing their services during even informal social situations or personal conversations.

For example, at a party an insurance salesperson states, "I am an insurance agent." A couple of people that he meets that night might just happen to need insurance. A second person says, "I am a writer," and who knows, maybe an agent will approach (which, admittedly, is more likely if you are in Los Angeles or New York). Even if that doesn't happen initially, you will have claimed your ambition in the present tense, the first step towards acting on it. Eventually, you will believe what you say aloud and engage in actions that strengthen your identity as a writer. If you can say it, you can do it (see Step Seven).

Many artists respond sheepishly when asked, "What do you do?" or, "What is your work?" These aspiring writers (or painters, actors, musicians) dig their hands into their pockets, bow their heads, shuffle imaginary pebbles beneath their feet, and offer barely audible responses, similar to chirps of a little bird: "I'm a, uh, a writer." Chirp, chirp.

Next time someone asks, "What do you do?" toss your shoulders back, inhale, expand your chest and exclaim, "I am a writer." If you believe you are a writer, you will become one, particularly as you develop the capacity to discipline yourself. If you have not already done so, begin creating your writer identity today. Own it.

Step Two:
Study and practice your craft.

Each day or week, read about your craft, screenwriting (or any of the arts). Study testimonials. Purchase and consume books on writing, particularly ones penned by writers (for example, *Bird by Bird* by Anne Lamott; *On Writing* by Stephen King; *How to Write Science Fiction or Fantasy* by Orson Scott Card; or *The Faith of a Writer* by Joyce Carol Oates). Experiment with, explore, and practice their suggestions and develop your ideas and daily regimens.

Musicians play music. Painters paint. Writers write. But more than that: musicians practice scales and combinations, gaining dexterity, counting beats and listening to gradations of tone; painters learn by experimenting with color, line, shape and perspective; writers compose for particular purposes, selecting appropriate genres, conventions, and stylistics for intended audiences. These artists engage daily with their craft until experiments become repertoire and part of their inventory of skills.

For example, I offered Will advice, "When you are auditioning or working towards a commercial, television show, or feature film, you must still act." This means, take a class; or perform in a local play; or select a monologue and practice before a mirror. Engaging daily in work that contributes to becoming an actor is how to stay sharp, articulate, and ready for the next role and opportunity. Similarly, writers experiment with metaphors, work on describing characters or constructing dialogue, read manuscripts aloud and listen for rhythm and cadence, and envision how scenes unfold, locating moments of dramatic tension, irony and conflict.

Young or inexperienced writers wait for heavenly or spiritual inspiration to write. Or they wait for the next "great idea" to mystically present itself before putting pen to paper or clicking away at the keyboard. These writers often believe they first have to think—or discover golden lines—to write, or that they must sit before a keyboard or notepad and cogitate until their brains form pearls of wisdom or insight that invoke or shape a script. They wonder, "If I think hard enough, won't wisdom, or characters, or epiphanies emerge?" Experienced writers approach the task differently.

Although initial planning occurs, professional writers "write to think." Seasoned writers begin with an idea or character, and through writing discover more about that idea, or character, or scene. While writing, I have observed how quickly the brain navigates my fingers into collaboratively composing drafts of description or dialogue, even if the initial pages are ugly.

According to a famous study by educator Janet Emig of students' composing processes, writing is a mode of learning; therefore, as we write we are generating opportunities for learning, thinking, and creating.

15

However, in order to shape drafts into distinct plots and characters, writers must discipline themselves to sit, listen, and observe, and then—through the act of writing—further explore potential sequences of a scene or story and qualities of a character.

Carve out time each day to write.

Picasso claimed he sat before an easel six hours every day, even if he did not mix a color or pick up a paintbrush. He said, "Art is ten percent inspiration and ninety percent perspiration." Yes, sitting for six hours is challenging, but you can learn how, and that discipline will encourage you to produce. There is no secret or luck for writers. A very successful friend of mine once remarked, "I worked fourteen hours a day, seven days a week, and got really lucky."

Work at your craft daily. Carve out time each day to write. Begin sitting at your desk for one hour a day and build your capacity to six hours. The regimen will give you structure (and patience) to create an inventory of manuscripts. If your circumstances demand, begin with five minutes and build from there; but, work consistently each day—the cumulative total of minutes, eventually hours, will determine what you accomplish.

Initially, this task may feel mentally and physically insurmountable. However, notice the amount of time you already spend at the computer. I know a woman who is a brilliant writer — she has more talent in her fingernails than I will have in several lifetimes, yet she rarely writes. I asked her why she finds it difficult to write. She says she doesn't have time, yet she spends an average of four hours each day uncontrollably surfing the Internet to peruse various interests. She has no trouble meandering through a range of Web sites for hours but finds typing one page of a composition challenging—even on subjects she knows well and wants to capture in writing. Because of a "lack of time," she accomplishes nothing as a writer.

You may not have six hours to write each day, or even one hour. Therefore, take the bits of time you do have and write. Research has shown that productive writers are consistent: if they have only fifteen minutes on a particular day, they select a part of a manuscript and work on it, and this focused time builds and leads towards completing the script. You may need to begin with five minutes at a time, but that is thirty-five minutes for the week, which beats, "Someday, [sigh], I hope I have time to write."

Another person I know has wordsmith abilities rivaling prolific authors. The man can spin sentences into resonating golden thoughts. For years he's been telling me, "I'm going to get back into the writing game." However, he too spends an amazing amount of time on the Internet. Some mornings I pass his place and see him perched before the monitor. Later that evening, frozen in the same position, eyes riveted to the screen, he has demonstrated consistency and amazing focus, but no pages. I wonder how many pages he could have cranked out with even half of that time devoted to writing.

I encourage both of these people to write: "Try to spend a fifth of your Internet time typing some pages. See what happens." Although they claim, "I want to write," they decline my invitation or grow quiet, waiting for the voice of reason to dissipate and the possibilities to disappear. Although I don't fully understand the psychology behind the "whys" and "why not's" of people's motivation to write, or the apparent audacity and confidence necessary to write, I do know that many people believe that everything they write has to reflect perfection—even on first drafts. They appear stifled by fantasies of perfection and, ultimately, they retreat into their imaginary worlds of, "If I had more time, I could really write something great—I just know it." But they don't believe it, or fear that their best effort may not be enough, and they stop writing.

I adhere to Anne Lamott's theory on writing "shitty first drafts," described in her book *Bird by Bird*:

For me and most of the writers I know, writing is not rapturous. In fact, the only way I can get anything written at all is to write a really, really shitty first draft. The first draft is the child's draft, where you let it all pour out and then let it romp all over the place, knowing that no one is going to see it and that you can shape it later." (22)

Lamott's philosophy liberated me. I start and finish an initial draft without looking back, or criticizing. When I've completed a draft of a screenplay, I begin to rewrite, layer, re-envision, and write more.

A literary agent once told me that his only frustration is that his "writer clients" don't write. It's difficult to critique even a "shitty" first draft of a screenplay when it is stuffed inside someone's head, which appears safer for some aspiring writers; however, the initial draft encourages you to explore what is there and how to shape or sculpt it into your vision, or one that will emerge from the cyclical process of writing.

My personal technique is to draw several boxes on paper and scribble words or thoughts in them. One idea leads to another and suddenly I have many boxes linked towards a story. My Emmy-nominated television movie, "The Simple Life of Noah Dearborn" (starring Sidney Poitier), started with a box. Inside the box I wrote, "Live forever if you love what you do." I eventually created a character that loved his craft (carpentry) and lived far beyond one hundred years.

Step Three:
Do something each day to advance your craft.

D o something toward your craft each day, even if it is only reading about a writer (or actor), or reading (or viewing) the work of this person. As a writer, write (if you are an actor, act). Purposefully engaging in work towards your goal each day becomes habitual, and the daily attention to a project, regimen, and discipline builds confidence in your capacity to perform, to complete writing tasks. Long-term projects are chunked into manageable parts.

When we "chip away," shapes
emerge from the vision we initiated.

I call this approach my "chipping away theory." Each day a writer should chip away at his or her goal: complete one page, call one agent, read one book, among other actions, that will lead to a first draft and towards a completed screenplay. Similar to a sculptor, grip your metaphoric chisel and hammer and clink away, forming and clarifying the vision you have for a particular idea or character, or preparing for your next steps in the process of shaping your vision. Turning to another metaphor, you may feel like you are racing around a circular track at warped speed yet reaching no particular destination, but the focus and repetition of the work will eventually lead you to pause and notice that you have completed a screenplay, or a pilot for a television series.

When we "chip away," shapes emerge from the vision we initiated. Or, to invoke a twenty-first century technology metaphor, and to revisit the idea that writing leads to thinking or clarifying a vision, we set our global positioning system for a destination and begin wandering through a maze of streets and buildings, uncertain whether or not the brains behind the voice have any idea about the road construction or the exact location of the address we typed in. However, as long as we continue driving, staying alert for key signs, we will eventually arrive. Remaining focused on a writing project daily, even when we're doing other things, leads us to complete the manuscript or screenplay. Staying focused can be easier if our vocation is located within the industry of writing.

At times, we may have to work at jobs unrelated to our craft. Obviously, you need money that provides the resources you need or demand. However, If you want to write screenplays for a living, I suggest finding work in a related area, or turning daily work into potential scenes or characters. Focus your energy and move towards your goal of writing screenplays, task-by-task, step-by-step, observation-by-observation. We can practice this approach even with our avocations.

Consider this metaphor that comes from my training in Tae Kwon Do.

When inexperienced students practice a new form (or *poomse* or *kata*, i.e., a series of prescribed movements), they often bob their head up and down before continuing towards the next movement, until they learn how to maintain a consistent head level (which is required by many forms), eyes focused on performing the next moves with power, agility and grace. When students maintain appropriate balance and focus, they exhibit "good form," improve their performance and efficiency of movement, and eventually they achieve their next rank or belt.

Similar to martial artists focusing on their form over time, writers stay centered on tasks of writing. However, coupled with increasing their time and energy towards their craft, many writers consider finding work related to the industry they want to work in, as other artists do. For example, my son is a talented musician. When he was in high school he wanted to earn extra money to buy a guitar and drum kit. I told him to forget about the local fast food chain; instead, I suggested that he sweep floors at a recording studio and discover how the business works there from the ground level—daily opportunities that would encourage him to focus on his music and the industry. Sometimes kids do listen to good advice, and he did. And it made a difference for his career.

Yet, there are jobs we must do that appear irrelevant to writing (and your circumstances might demand you retain your current employment), but we can use these experiences to our advantage as writers. For example, if your boss (or parent, or spouse, etc.) admonishes you to complete an undesirable task, why spend all day moaning about it, or neglecting it, to prove a point, which detracts from your writing. Instead, observe the situation, the characters and obvious conflict. Envision possibilities that the scene presents. You may be able to incorporate the experience in your writing. Instead of discovering yourself mired in controversy, observe and gather experiences and put them into scripts. Instead of viewing life as a "daily grind," see opportunities to advance your craft and career, much the way other writers have done, such as J. K. Rowling, a single mother who created time to write *Harry Potter*.

Step Four:
Study and emulate a writer you admire.

Find a writer you wish to emulate, past or present, for the purposes of learning. Study his or her path to success. Observe key hurdles or mistakes the person overcame or made, particularly the key opportunities she or he created. Study the writer's processes, manuscripts, and revisions. I once read an inspirational interview with Sue Grafton. She spoke openly about her journey from writing screenplays to embarking on a path as a prolific novelist. Her words triggered the courage for me to start my first novel.

When Will first told me he wanted to be an actor, I told him to study the greats: Freeman, Pacino, Fishburne, Nicholson, Hackman, Di Nero, Streep, Penn, Oldman, Redgrave, Cheadle, Lewis, Bates, Hoffman, Swank, among others.

Zoom in on one or two great writers in genres that interest you. Crime stories intrigue me, and there is a saying that inspires me: "If you are a writer and want to know what you should be writing, write what you read in your spare time." You choose. Before bed, I often read Bruen, or Chandler, Leonard, Crais, Burke, or a few other terrific crime writers. Reading their work is like studying and incorporating complicated sheet music into a musician's repertoire: I listen to the rhythm, tone, pace and sense of story and sample and play the notes through my writing.

However, I do more than read other writers' manuscripts. I study their biographies, reading about their hardships as well as successes. How did they accomplish the work that led to their success? Yes, some people appear to have been graced by the writing gods, but they have also put themselves in the position to recognize and embrace opportunities, and they work hard and experience failures before achieving success. Research has demonstrated that writing is not a state of grace; it is learned within social contexts, and people who practice improve.

Seasoned writers learn more from mistakes, or perceived errors, than from their successes, and I discovered how to turn problems into opportunities during my first writing job for a television show. The initial episode I wrote was laden with errors and structural problems. One of the producers barked at me in the writers' room. I took the long, torturous, journey back to my office to start over. After a few minutes, the showrunner (or the creator) of the popular television show "The Shield," walked into my office, closed the door, and told me that the most problematic episodes often end up being the best. I stared at him, dumbfounded.

He described how every part of a show, from writers and editors to the showrunner and line producers, collaboratively pull problematic shows together. His experience as a writer led me to trust the process; from him and the other more seasoned writers on the show, I was learning how "shitty first drafts" can develop through joint effort. Many of my colleagues helped shape the script into one of the most watched episodes of the series, and the lead actor on the show later told me was his favorite of the year.

Ask people who have written on a television show, they will tell you that the learning happens during moments of crisis. The rally cry galvanizes the set, writers' room, art department, and editing bay, and the collaboration among the parts creates something out of apparent chaos, or shit. It seems that little is learned during periods of serenity, and writers who had been there before helped me understand this, and I learned from them how most published writing is collaborative.

"You have to drink a lot of bad wine
to know good wine."

Before moving to Hollywood to begin my writing career, I was a vintner in Napa Valley. I interviewed Mondavi, Phelps, Luper, and Draper, a few of the legendary winemakers. I asked them what mistakes they had made. All of these men gladly took a moment from their busy schedules to share insights from their winemaking experiences with an enthusiastic green horn. Sometimes if you ask honest, thoughtful questions, the greats are happy to answer. These expert winemakers agreed, "You have to drink a lot of bad wine to know good wine." And, implicitly, you have to make bad wine before you learn how to make good wine.

I learned from listening to and watching them. Sometimes my hasty decisions or conclusions proved ignorant, but I learned. For example, one of my mentors in the wine business had only friends who were somehow connected to his winery. His associates were salespersons, winemakers, restaurateurs, and wine and food critics. Naïvely, I viewed my mentor as calculating, unethical and insincere. However, years later, after he had earned the respect of his peers and built an empire close to a billion dollars, I realized that he was entrepreneurial, savvy, strategic. He had made mistakes, but he learned from them, and his friends often remarked on his perseverance and loyalty.

I am not suggesting that your only friends should be writers, editors, producers, and directors; I am suggesting that you gather knowledge from the practices, mistakes and achievements of successful writers; learn the business; and discover the shortcuts, secrets, and strategies of prolific writers. Minimally, your observations will provide you with unique perspectives and experiences that you can transform to make your own.

Step Five:
Do the work to be great.

Strive to be greater than the person you most admire in your craft. Ambitious? Yes, but if you work harder and smarter, you might become greater than your heroes. Prominent and successful people work hard to achieve what they have, and learning from their actions—and pushing those boundaries—can help you establish a foundation and lead you towards your own greatness. For example, if basketball Hall of Famer Michael Jordan shot five thousand jump shots a day, then shoot seven thousand. If Albert Pujols, of the St. Louis Cardinals, swings the bat one thousand times, then swing two thousand. Similar analogies can be made with famous musicians, artists and actors. If you aspire to greatness, do what the great ones did, and then do more.

In Tae Kwon Do, learning to kick is important. At first, I obediently followed along with the class and performed the ten or twenty repetitions on each leg for each type of kick demanded by the instructor. However, as I observed the power and "pop" in the kicks of advanced students and my instructors, I learned that repetitions during class were only a fraction of the number of kicks they performed each day. I began to push and kick until exhaustion; then, I kicked more.

As a screenwriter I believed ten pages a day would suffice, then one day David Mamet, the Pulitzer Prize winning playwright, director, and screenwriter, arrived on set of the television show "The Unit" with a finished draft of a play that he composed over the weekend. Astonished, I asked, holding the manuscript: "You wrote this in one weekend?" Through his confirmation, Mamet demonstrated a possibility and way of working that I had not considered. So I decided to write a pilot for television over a weekend, and I did. That script later sold.

One of the main aspects of this principle is this: whether or not you become "greater" than someone as talented as David Mamet is less important than learning from the people who have come before you and engaging in actions that propel you towards your own greatness.

Jay Leno once said, "While everyone was sleeping or partying, I was getting ahead." This resonated with me and increased my capacity to ignore beautiful weather (or a concert, or the "party of the century") and stay inside and write. Leno's statement validated my belief that sitting and grinding out pages of a script would pay off. It did. People who demand or expect instant gratification rarely understand that gratification will come tenfold when you achieve your goals; although though the steps or processes may demand way more disciplined time than you had presumed.

To further illustrate this point, one of my favorite stories featured "partying habits" of a few successful television writer/producers. They were asked, "Is it true that you all throw the most Incredible parties every week?" One of the writers responded (I'm paraphrasing), "Yes, because we spent years inside only writing. Now we have some catching up to do." The writers had made tremendous sacrifices. They were able to stay focused on their goals, their "eyes on the prize." Their effort and discipline continued to pay dividends: they created more freedom to plan for and work on other projects—and to travel and party.

Step Six:
Set daily goals.

Everything I have accomplished professionally started out on a piece of paper. I doodle, journal, and write lofty ambitions. As I mentioned before, I write seeds of ideas and goals in boxes (see Step Two). When I begin mapping a plan on paper—words and scribbles in dozens of boxes—those ideas and goals appear doable, and I become invigorated.

My vintner career started from a journal entry, in a small box, that read, "Make wine." Before that, I worked as a wine and food critic and restaurant reviewer, a vocation that started from scribbles in my journal, a box that read, "Write about wine." Years later, I wrote an idea for a novel on a piece of paper and it became my first big screenplay speculation ("spec") sale. The box read "Card Shark," an idea that developed into a script, "Jacks or Better," that Disney bought. The story is about a card shark who planned to hustle money from a group of wealthy senior citizens; however, after he got to know them, he fell in love with them as if they were the mothers and fathers he never had. Although the manuscript remains archived, the check was happily cashed, and I turned towards other goals and ideas scribbled in boxes.

Words spread into actions.

Words spread into actions. Set your goals each day. Write them down. The physical task and visual result will help you see what you want to accomplish as a screenwriter. I read somewhere, "Goals are the deadlines of your dreams." Similar to Step One ("own it"), you are writing what you plan to accomplish, the crucial step towards engaging in your work as a writer.

You might find it useful to reflect on a day's work and jot your goals for the next day. Then upon waking, read those goals, envision them and get to work. There are many days when I feel that I have accomplished little, yet when I return home and open my list of goals for that day, I realize I have accomplished two or three of them. When I was younger, I started the school year by listing goals and mailing them to myself. At the end of the year I would open the letter and see how I did. I was rarely disappointed because I had turned the vision into action. Many times I added items to my list that I had unwittingly accomplished.

People write grocery or "to do" lists, purchase the items or perform the tasks and think of these actions as just "part of the daily grind." Yet, writing your professional and personal goals encourages you to engage in practices that lead you to reach your dreams as a writer. Goals are not only the deadlines of our dreams, they are also the grocery or "to do" lists of our lives.

Step Seven:
Say your goals and dreams aloud.

Say or chant your goals and dreams out loud. What you say you become. "Done" is what I say when I list a goal—even before I have literally begun the work to accomplish it. If you can see the goal and say it, you can do it. Christians say, "The word made flesh"; Buddhists say, "You are what you say and think." What you say becomes who you are, even though the process may be initially imperceptible. If you habitually complain, you become a complainer. When you say or chant, "I am a writer," you become a writer.

A very successful talk show host once said to me in the green room, "You know, Sterling, every actor who appeared on my show and said, 'I will be a star,' is now a star." Conversely, ninety-nine percent of the people who said "No way," never found a way. If you want further validation of how words manifest into action, just ask any divorced person about the initial steps that led towards his or her marital demise: one of them was the mention of the word *divorce*. The idea became a possibility, and then a reality.

All of us were prompted or "hardwired" to become who we perceive ourselves to be by the words of friends, teachers, parents, and siblings, among others—some studies suggest that even our names influence our actions and beliefs. The words from these people contributed to the path we may or may not have chosen for ourselves; yet, somehow their words contributed to self-perceptions that shape our actions.

For example, a family member often told me that I was lazy and a failure, and my actions often proved that I believed it. Many times, I would approach a goal but somehow sabotage my efforts. One day, I read something that altered my learned, self-deprecating perspective: "People are not failures. People only fail at certain things." The change of the tide in my life began as I embraced this precept. I realized that I'm not lazy or a failure as a person, although I have failed at certain tasks or relationships.

In sports, athletes are considered successful for what they achieve, not for periodically failing at related tasks. For example, Michael Jordan scored many game winning shots and helped his team win multiple championships, yet he missed many more shots than he made. Babe Ruth hit 714 home runs but struck out nearly twice as often (1,330 times). Jerry Rice caught more touchdown passes than any other receiver in the National Football League (197), but he also dropped many passes—early in his career he was viewed as an unreliable receiver. Occasionally, professional tennis player Roger Federer hits the ball into the net instead of over it; Olympian soccer star Mia Hamm missed shots on goal, yet all these athletes are considered successful for their body of work.

Of course, these athletes represent some of the greatest in their sports and people point to their heroics. Other successful athletes are recognized for their one or two mistakes, yet they excelled and their greatness becomes a matter of perspective. Therefore, For example, Bill Buckner committed an error in the 1986 World Series that contributed to the loss of a key game; yet, in twenty-two big league seasons, he slugged nearly 3,000 hits (2,715) and 200 home runs (174), and he demonstrated consistency as a hitter with a near .300 batting average (.289). He exemplified a consummate professional through his work ethic and career achievement; he was not a failure—even his responses to ridicule reflected his professionalism. As Buckner often did, these athletes endured criticisms but forged their efforts around their plans and goals.

"Plan now or you will become a part of someone else's plan."

In high school, a substitute teacher stood in front of the class one day and said, "Plan now or you will become a part of someone else's plan." These words smacked me. I was a sixteen years old alien. My brain was forming neurological pathways; my hormones raged. Yet, somehow the words of that teacher penetrated my teenage-bullet-proof-Kevlar-of-self-righteousness and importance: "Plan now or become a part of someone else's plan," I repeated. Stunned, then reflective, I started planning as I walked home that day.

Over my life, I've changed directions at times, but my approach has a consistent pattern: write my goals, state them aloud *repeatedly*, and engage the practices that lead me to accomplish them. One of the key qualities of my success has been to engage in the necessary work and complete projects I start, even when I was younger. For example, in eighth grade I decided I wanted to attend college on scholarship, I did. That same year I saw my first Bruce Lee movie (*Fists of Fury*). During my freshman year in college, I enrolled at a local martial art studio and trained and earned a black belt (I hold a fifth degree black belt in Tae Kwon Do).

I met Joseph Phelps and decided I wanted to be a winemaker. I did. I read a script and decided to write one. I finished. All of these accomplishments were stepping-stones to my next goals, although I could not have understood that then. For example, I did not know I wanted to be a writer when I started learning martial arts. However, completing my black belt freed me to accomplish something else, then something else, and then something else. Complete one writing goal and you will see how many others follow, and this approach becomes habitual and helps you build capacity to achieve your goals as a writer.

Many people rely on others to set goals for them. In fact, if you do not set goals, someone else will eventually do that for you, as the teacher suggested. And, of course, those goals may be related to that person's agenda, not yours. Create a plan and set goals towards it, or make yourself part of the plans of others and achieve the goals they set for you your own. Write your goals and, like the late singer and performer James Brown once said, "Say it loud!" *I will write ten pages a day and complete this script in one month!*

Step Eight:
Create time with inspirational people.

F ind and interact with inspirational people. If most of us could retrieve the time we have spent with negative, uninspired bores, we could have written a *War and Peace*-type novel, multiple volumes. Because of social and economic circumstances it may be impossible, at times, to pry yourself from naysayers and oppressors. But observe your interactions with others and, if necessary, plot strategies to create change. We often assess the potential of others and note their apparent failings, yet we are often blind to our own similar dilemmas.

Years ago, when a few dinosaurs still roamed the earth, I was studying at HB Studios with Uta Hagen and Herbert Bergoff. In one particular scene-study class, there was a young woman as talented as she was beautiful. Her beauty glowed like Angelina Jolie's and her talent seemed to approach a young, venerable Meryl Streep's. We all leaned forward, mouths open, in marvel of this protégée. Her life promised unbound potential. The red carpet unfurled before her in preparation for her waltz towards fame and the award of her star at Hollywood and Vine. However, one day as we arrived for class, I noticed this young woman slumped on a step, crying. The doors to the classroom were locked, so I wandered over and bravely asked her what was wrong?

She murmured that she was going home, back to Nebraska, because her "grease-monkey boyfriend," who couldn't care less about her career ambitions, had instructed her to drop the "acting thing" and get to his home and become barefoot and pregnant, her "rightful lot in life." Unfortunately, Mr. Enlightenment swayed her because she did leave and never returned. Once a year, during the Academy Awards, I often wonder what would have happened if she had stayed. The world never got the chance to see the shining star that opted to extinguish her light and trudge back to the cornfields of Nebraska. What if she had dumped the boyfriend and surrounded herself with encouraging people, or gritted her teeth and moved beyond the vision someone else had for her?

> *Find and observe people who are*
> *diligent and inspired, particularly writers*
> *or other artists.*

What if Miles Davis, John Lennon, Jimi Hendrix, or Billie Holliday had been told to quit, and did? The hallowed space they each created would have been lost, indistinguishable gaps in music history. I am sure there have been greats we have never gotten to see, hear, or read because the negativity or cruelty of others choked their potential. Luckily the great ones, like Davis et al. didn't listen, and shared with us their uncanny talents that we've enjoyed for generations.

Find and observe people who are diligent and inspired, particularly writers or other artists. Find ways to spend time with or around them. In terms of a running metaphor, keep pace with them, observe their form and technique, or ways they work, or strive to outrun them. Limit the contact with people who drag you down, or clamp their fangs into you and suck out the vitality, energy, and idealism you need to accomplish your goals. Get rid of the time drains. Replace them with opportunities to hear inspirational people urge you forward as a screenwriter, ones who say, "Yes, you can!"

Yes, you may lose people when you focus and work hard, or reshape relationships. Ninety percent of the actors and actresses we watch have put in countless hours of rehearsals and auditions. To get to where they are, they had to put on blinders and stay centered on their goals. The millions of dollars that famous actors make are often not enough to mend relationships with parents, siblings, or other loved ones who took their absence as a form of rejection or selfishness. However, engaging in the work, including the interactions with positive people—which will lead you towards your goals and dreams as a screenwriter—includes negotiating or assessing the value of your relationships.

If your commitments with others are loving and strong, built on solid foundations, you will be able to carve out the necessary time and space to write towards your goals—that is what supportive people want for their significant others or family members or friends; if the relationships are strained and require arbitration, the work you generate and commit to may help resolve some of those difficult situations. If not, you will face decisions similar to the budding actress who retreated to the apparent safety of the known, even though the latter reflected someone else's dream.

I too have had to block out naysayers and oppressors. For example, after I told the close relative (mentioned earlier) that I wanted to be a writer, he rattled me with doubt: "You're throwing away your life." A few years later, at the party organized to celebrate one of my successes as a writer, he stood and offered a toast, concluding ironically with, "I always encouraged him." If that were remotely true, I might have written my first novel years earlier.

One of my English professors in college told me that I had "no shot at becoming a writer." These seminal moments stoked my fire and generated motivation in me to succeed. To be a writer (actor, musician, painter), rejection must in some respects fuel your fire. Certainly, if rejection devastates you, do not become a writer. Each day I must put up with some form of disapproval or criticism. Producers, agents, studios, and networks are all foot soldiers seemingly programmed to crack the self-esteem of writers. Because of my own background, I will never be the person to belittle aspiring writers' dreams of becoming successful—and paid—screenwriters.

I come from a context where I appeared to have no chance at becoming a successful writer. I was born poor, fatherless, and homeless, and no one envisioned that I would grow up to earn a living writing screenplays. Yet, I had the faith and ambition to try. When my students make comments about the impossibility of becoming a successful screenwriter, I encourage them by asking, "Is writing a screenplay any harder than negotiating, for example, a marriage or raising children?" I guarantee you that maintaining a marriage and raising children are a hundred times more difficult than writing screenplays, as are other challenging situations.

It is interesting that more than eighty percent of my students claim that they plan on getting married and having kids, yet less than ten percent of them unequivocally plan on becoming a paid screenwriter. Of course, many of us are encouraged—even inspired—to marry and have children. Using this logic, here is another reason to state aloud your intentions as a writer. Say you are a writer, surround yourself with others who encourage you as a writer, and your chances of succeeding rise dramatically. (Note: If you are motivated only by naysayers, go directly to Step Thirteen!)

Step Nine:
Find a mentor.

Find a mentor. Some people who are successful are generous with their time and experience. Not all, but some. Find them. Do not ask them for help, just guidance. Get pointed in the right or productive direction. For example: rather than ask a mentor for permission to meet his or her agent (which is socially inappropriate), ask, "What is your best advice on how to approach an agent?" Often I am surprised by the willingness of some of the giants to encourage others. True, many successful people are unapproachable. Their apparent desire to be seen as great or eccentric, or worshipped by adoring fans, changed their availability from a willingness to share insights to deliberate, self-congratulatory aloofness. However, there are giants who believe, as I do, that once you take the elevator up, you must send it back down for others to follow.

Approaching potential mentors can be as simple as just asking (as long as it doesn't include incessantly calling them on the phone, stalking, or sending rude emails). For example, one day while I was writing on the television show "The Unit" with David Mamet (the showrunner), Mamet walked in followed by a young man. Mamet introduced him as a college student whom he was mentoring. We were astounded that someone as prodigious as Mamet would make time for an outside mentee. Later, we asked the kid, "How did you get Mamet to agree to mentor you?" The kid shrugged, "I asked."

There are several people who have asked me to mentor them. People have different needs, and mentors are no different. As a mentor to aspiring writers, I have only one rule: the mentoring cannot overshadow the time I must spend working on and monitoring my own career. Yet, there is nothing more rewarding than giving back to the field that provided opportunities for my success. A few of my screenwriting students have gone on to far exceed the modicum of success I have accomplished. I am proud of them all. Happiness and success do not decrease when shared.

Step Ten:
Make your bed.

Make your bed every day. If all things go wrong, you have accomplished at least one task early in the day. A mentor of mine once encouraged me to make my bed each day, and I thought he was crazy, or that he had been smoking the pipe. Neither was true, although his advice seemed dull and uninspiring. After I told my mentor this, he said, "If all else fails that day— and you do nothing more, you will have accomplished at least one task that day, making the bed." Maybe make some coffee too.

What this wise old Jedi encouraged me to discover was that accomplishing one task creates a domino effect. There is a saying I believe is true, "If you want something done, give it to a busy man." When I have little to do, I accomplish very little. Usually if I have only one thing to do and the entire day to do it, it doesn't get done. Suddenly, menial tasks rise in importance (e.g., "I've got to find that picture of my grandmother before I write!"). However, when my list of projects appears over-whelming, I produce. Idleness, one of the seven deadly sins during the medieval ages, is the enemy.

Basically, learn to do something well that you do not particularly like to do. If I rise, mill about pondering what to eat and the purpose of life, leave my bed crumpled, and meander outside towards the day, I have ignored an initial task that prepares me mentally for the day's writing. However, if I begin by making my bed, which I've learned to enjoy, I am started.

Step Eleven:
Think good thoughts.

Think and enact good thoughts. Every day, envision where you want to be—see the place. Offer your god thanks, and ask for help to stay the course. If you do not believe in a god, the simple quantum physics of positive thinking still applies. Positive thoughts propel you toward your goals; negative thoughts restrain or oppress you.

Ralph Waldo Emerson writes: "And so of cheerfulness, or a good temper, the more it is spent, the more of it remains. Cheerfulness is not the same as frivolousness; cheerfulness is born of a fighting spirit. Frivolousness is the reverse side of cowardly escape." Cheerfulness is an action and, at times, even an act; however, it is also a stance, a position from which to work towards your daily goals. As Emerson also stated, "power dwells with cheerfulness; hope puts us in a working mood."

Every sunrise presents us with opportunity and challenge, and a question. Shall we face the sunny side of the street and see opportunity, or shall we turn towards the dark clouds and fear and despair? Like many artists, I lean towards the latter, yet I have learned to embrace the former.

At one point in my career I was so maudlin and racked with doubt, I approached a friend for advice. We had run the streets as young men, from playing sports to following pretty faces; we shared secrets, fantasies, and fears. When my friend caught lightening-in-the-bottle and became a huge Hollywood agent to many noted stars, I asked him for help. He glanced and then stared at me: "Dude, I can't help you, man," he said, pursing his lips, "You are way too depressed." He turned away and seemed to ignore me at a critical time.

It took me years to forgive my friend; but it took me even longer to realize he was right, at the time. There was no way he could have set up any meetings for me: I was moping around with storm clouds over my head, like a cartoon frame of Charlie Brown in Peanuts. Any contacts or introductions probably would have resulted in rejection. I would have burned bridges and reflected poorly on my friend.

Every sunrise presents us with opportunity and challenge, and a question.

I learned an important lesson when approaching potential employers, when it comes to picking you or the other person, the prize will go to the one who is liked the most, the one who "fits." That is, when talent appears equal, the default is personality. The business of writing scripts for television and film is collaborative. If you do not want to collaborate, play solitaire or chess on your computer. Without cheerfulness there is little strength for the interactions with others during the negotiated and challenging process of weaving together personalities towards a common goal: a successful script. Strive to advance brightly and cheerfully. Think good thoughts. It's not a Cheshire grin that invites good will; rather, the daily freshness of your vigor and willingness to work with others helps creates potential for effective collaboration and success.

Step Twelve:
Be selfish.

Being selfish sounds ironic, particularly after reading Step Eleven, and this suggestion is contentious. For example, a celebrated sports columnist and commentator responded to a statement by a fan who blasted a famous athlete as "selfish." The columnist/commentator acknowledged a rationale for the fan's perception, but he explained that the phrase "great athlete" implies selfishness: focusing on one's self is a prerequisite to becoming great. Obviously, perspective is key here.

Anyone who chooses to spend eight or more hours a day training, eating appropriate foods, studying film, and engaging in other demands, must become selfish to some degree in order to achieve his or her goals. World-class athletes rarely have time to mow the lawn, buy stamps, wash the car, or take care of the household pets. World-class athletes leave in the morning and return in the evening. Parents, relatives, teachers, and significant others often give world-class athletes a free pass. The athletes earn this free pass for many reasons: potential financial rewards, the voyeuristic nature and pleasure of watching someone train towards success, the recognition of the physical demands to achieve or excel at high levels, among other reasons.

Every two years as we watch the Olympics and listen to announcers recount the training regimen of athletes, we do not accuse, for example, th gold medal winner of a 100 meters of being selfish for training eight to ten hours a day. Rather, we call it discipline, sacrifice, and determination. However, when a writer writes all day or night (or a painter paints, or a musician plays for long periods of time), he or she is often considered self-absorbed, narcissistic, eccentric or selfish.

My ex-wife used to stroll into the room while I was working on a script, the deadline closing in, and ask rhetorically if I had forgotten to mow the lawn—stopping my intense process. Glancing at her, I would ask, "If I were a surgeon, would you trounce into the operating room and ask me if I had forgotten to mow the lawn?" Hmmm. However, I understand that "working" at home raises questions. Many people physically "go to work," implying that they leave the home and drive to another building, a place where accomplishing household chores is impossible. But I usually write at home, so can't I just stop for an hour and push the mower back and forth, or dash to the store and pick up some tampons and toilet paper, or chop vegetables, or other work that needs to get done?

Why not? Because I am working, which was the agreement I had with my ex-wife. Even when I wander around the house, I am thinking, incubating on an idea, character, or plot for a script. Writers must create boundaries in order to accomplish their work. Of course, preferably you will negotiate with your significant other and together create a productive schedule and workspace.

By selfish, I am not implying that you create or take opportunities to be rude or cruel. Rather, I suggest clarifying your writing goals, seeing and saying them aloud (see Step Seven), and engaging in the work that will lead you to achieve your objectives. You must carve out time (see Step Two). As you wander through the house, or sit perched before your computer, people around you might resent your apparent reluctance to do mundane chores. However, the checks earned from your focus, sacrifice, and discipline will help in the long run. And don't forget to remind them that you made the bed (see Step Ten).

Step Thirteen:
Find and use sustainable motivation.

In my screenwriting classes, I tell a story of how I chose to become a writer. As I mentioned earlier (see Step Eight), at nineteen years old I was told by one of my English professors that I was "never going to be a writer." That seminal moment angered and motivated me to dedicate myself to finding a way to become a writer. On the surface it may appear that I sought to turn poison into medicine, or base metal into gold. On some level, both are true. I swallowed a negative comment and used it to fuel my desire to learn how to write; and even though the process was painful, I dedicated myself to the craft of writing.

For years, the negative comments fueled my motivation, until I lost the passion to prove myself to the naysayer I mentioned in Step Eight. I learned that negative comments may serve to spirit or inflame motivation, and spawn goals for a year—even ten years or twenty years, but eventually the negativity dissipates, or burns out. Even so, when you have the money, the car, the house, the bank account, and spiritual peace, those naysayers will rarely change their opinions about you, and you will not easily forget them or their influence.

Ironically, the day you realize that you no longer need their negativity as fuel, you begin to suffer repercussions. For example, the family member that I have spent nearly a lifetime trying to please, to love and approve of me, still can't (for reasons beyond my control). My desire for his love dwindled. But when I shut down "the program" that spurred me into action—the psychologically perverse need for his approval and my willingness to view his negative responses as attention, all my other programs shut down: that is, I stopped writing, exercising, reading, and praying. I discovered that "the program" to garner approval operated all my other programs; and my desire to write, read, golf, and exercise disappeared.

Metaphorically, I had to examine my DNA and reconstruct why and how I commit to my work, particularly as a writer. Jettisoning the negative motivation, which spirited emotional growth, stifled my motivation in the areas of my life built on it. Therefore, I uncovered the need for *sustainable motivation*.

> *Our identity derives partly from our*
> *personal and professional interactions*
> *and work, particularly through exploring*
> *emotions and gaining insights into how*
> *and why we act the way we do.*

I needed to re-construct how to achieve what I desired as a writer. Chisel away the negativity you may be accustomed to living with and you may be left with a void. For me, detaching from the drive to gain approval from a significant other left me with only negative perceptions of myself. Our identity derives partly from our personal and professional interactions and work, particularly through exploring emotions and gaining insights into how and why we act the way we do. I learned that I needed to incorporate sustainable motivation in order to design and achieve the ambitious goals I had set; when that work emerges from positive, productive exploration, not from the pelting or lashings of others, I would be able to sustain it.

Who we are, at least how we perceive ourselves, can become rooted in our daily, conscious lives, particularly our disciplined work as screenwriters. I am not a psychologist or psychiatrist, but I know we must explore and discover sustainable motivation, which I have learned must include self-acceptance, love and vision. Through this perspective, I am now motivated to write for positive, intrinsic reasons, e.g., the collaborating with others on a film, envisioning and creating the story that I envision, sharing my lessons with others, and achieving the recognition of peers for doing the work I love.

Step Fourteen:
Know the difference between transfer and transform.

S ome people believe that if they can write in one genre they should be successful writing in any genre; or that if athletes are good in one sport, they should excel in other sports; or if musicians can play one instrument well, they can play others equally as well. Yes, it is logical that we can transfer knowledge and practices from one discipline to another. If you are All-America at volleyball, tennis, or soccer, you can learn to transfer the time, energy and dedication from one sport to another; of course, that transfer does not guarantee success or imply that the skills exercised successfully in one sport simply transfer to another.

I extend this assumption to non-athletic fields. For example, three hours of hitting baseballs, throwing footballs, shooting basketballs, at least metaphorically can transfer into three hours of reading, learning to write, or developing stories for screenplays. This simple logic implies that you can go from being a top fashion designer to a top poet, or novelist; or from being a top educator to a top actor or painter—that expertise in one discipline can act as a springboard to prowess in another discipline. However, it is more complicated.

The belief that writing "skills" are easily transferable to any context is based on a model of writing that implies that skills are autonomous, i.e., once you have developed skills, you can apply them to any context. So if I have learned to write academic essays—and I have earned "A's," or had them published in academic journals—then I should be successful as I begin to write poetry, or a screenplay, or a pilot for a television series, among other genres. However, the contexts in which these types of writings occur are often vastly different. Therefore, it is not simply transferring skills that we must learn; rather, we must go through a process of transforming those or similar skills into new, or less familiar, contexts, including reshaping knowledge of genre conventions and audience expectations for the purposes in which we write.

For another example, I turn again to sports. Mark Harmon, Ed Marinaro, and Jim Brown took outstanding football careers and transformed themselves into notable actors. They did not simply transfer skills learned in one area to another; instead, they had to transform their knowledge of, for example, "working hard" as an athlete through rigorous study and devotion to what it means to work hard as an actor. Intellectually, they may have understood the principle of *discipline* or *hard work*; however, the actions that constitute discipline or hard work in one area often differ from another area.

Therefore, they had to transform their knowledge and skills to another discipline—and learn the skills specific to that discipline, in this case, acting. For example, lifting weights, sprinting up and down the football field, learning to hit and get hit during arduous practice sessions helped these men to excel at football. But they had to transform these actions, now parts of an athletic metaphor for them, into similar but much different actions demanded by experts and practitioners of stage and film.

Performing at a high level in one field does not guarantee anything in another area.

> *Performing at a high level in one field does not guarantee anything in another area.*

Their athletic prowess may have helped them get through the acting door, but they did not just show up and say, "Put me down for three Emmy nominations and Academy Awards because we were *all-world* at playing football." Instead, they proved to themselves and others that they were willing to do the work it would take to learn the craft of acting, to prepare them for the screen. Their past athletic experiences may have instilled confidence in them but their transformations demanded work and commitment.

Performing at a high level in one field does not guarantee anything in another. For example, after a three-day, grueling black belt test, I believed that the rest of life was going to be a cakewalk. "How could life be much harder than that?" I pondered as a twenty-one year old. But sitting down, reading, thinking, and crafting my writing skills was not automatic—the discipline I had learned in Tae Kwon Do did not easily transfer to writing. I had to immerse myself in writing and learn how to transform the practice of Tae Kwon Do into the work of writing in order to become a disciplined screenwriter.

When I first broke into screenwriting there was a California gold rush into the acting field. Rap artists from California to New York were given lead roles in movies. This violated the belief system that I had about learning to do the work and achieving goals over time. How could these street poets be given carte blanche the opportunities to be movie stars, when noted Tony award-winning actors and actresses who had labored for years to hone their skills were ignored? Just because I had been a Tae Kwon Do champion did not give me to right to believe I could be a screenwriter based on the grace and power of my kicks, nor did it provide me the information and experience I needed to write daily, pitch scripts, negotiate, and rewrite and rewrite and rewrite.

I learned that sometimes we have to ignore apparent discrepancies and focus on our own work.

Now, rap artists are taking classes, doing the work and transforming—not transferring—their understanding of performing on the stage to the screen. As some of them (e.g., Ice Cube and Queen Latifah) have achieved success in the film industry, they are illustrating how they transformed themselves through learning and practicing the craft. Learning to write as a screenwriter demands similar transformative experiences by writers who have mainly written in other genres. And it demands that you have the audacity to believe you can, even as other writers in the TV writers' room stare at you and wonder, "How did she [or he] get through this door?"

Step Fifteen:
Be fearless.

"There are two basic motivating forces: fear and love. When we are afraid, we pull back from life. When we are in love, we open to all that life has to offer with passion, excitement, and acceptance. We need to learn to love ourselves first, in all our glory and our imperfections. If we cannot love ourselves, we cannot fully open to our ability to love others or our potential to create. Evolution and all hopes for a better world rest in the fearlessness and open-hearted vision of people who embrace life. "

- John Lennon

Be Fearless. Although I cannot provide you with an easy path to accepting and loving yourself (or others), I have learned that Lennon's advice is part of the puzzle of fear, and that accepting our imperfections as writers is another part.

Fear deflects our focus. We stumble and fall into survival mode, grasp at illusions or fantasies and ignore daily regimen or practices demanded for success. Of course, we might fear different things (I hate snakes; my business partner fears flying), but the response of fear deflates our resolve and vigor towards achieving our goals. Gavin de Becker wrote *The Gift of Fear*, a wonderful book; however, I wish he had entitled it *The Gift of Caution*. Fear paralyzes us; caution suggests acting with conscious or profound awareness. We must be present, know what is happening around us.

From my observations, the film business is a fear-based industry. No one wants to be the person held accountable for the failure of a film or television series, yet taking that initial risk is what contributed to many scripts becoming colossal hits. At one point on the journey of the following films to the screen, no one wanted to produce them: *Dances with Wolves*, *Home Alone*, and *Forrest Gump*. Therefore, many movies and television shows, such as these, were passed over, until someone with vision embraced risk and produced and directed these box office giants.

In my career, fear urged me to pass on two films, *Save the Last Dance* and *Hangover*. Both projects were offered to me, but my fear kept me from stepping up to the plate and taking my swings. When the producers presented the idea of a dance movie to me, I was afraid I would be uninspired because I had only cursory knowledge of the topic. I passed on the project. When *Hangover* was presented to me, I was too afraid to fail as a comedy writer—"I'm not a comedy writer," I reasoned. I only half-heartedly returned to the table with an idea, and the studio had no other choice but to pass on me.

Fear prevented me from putting my best foot forward. Fear paralyzed me and kept me from doing the thing that comes most natural for me, which is starting a project. This was unusual for me. Fear prevented me from being myself.

The challenge for me is not to start a project. The real challenge is to forge ahead and complete it. Every time I reach the middle of the screenplay or teleplay, I hear fearful and doubtful voices, "This is stupid," or, "No one is going to like this"; or, my personal favorite self-lashing, "You keep writing this crap and they are really going to find out that you are a fraud." But I recall what Woody Allen said: "Eighty percent of success is showing up."

So I show up at my writing desk each morning. Each day that I wake up with the boot of fear on my chest, I must lift that boot and hurl it as far away from me as I can. Fear no longer serves me. What serves me is courage. Fear begets more fear and courage begets more courage. It is now an easy choice for me to make, and to say aloud (see Step Seven).

As a result of being afraid, I know from experience that I may do nothing; but nothing is not what happens. When I do nothing from the result of fear, something else happens, often unanticipated, that is usually not in my favor. Trust me: ninety percent of the time these fear demons resonate in my head. They come from being told somewhere along the way that I was no good or that I would not succeed—at least I heard it that way.

However, somehow I eventually draw and raise that magical sword from its scabbard, slaying the "dragon fear," breathing fire into my confidence. During these moments, I recall what F. Scott Fitzgerald said: "You don't write because you want to say something: You write because you've got something to say."

I extend his quote: I don't write because I want to say something that I hope everyone likes; I write because I have something to say in the way only I can say it. I can't write worrying about pleasing everyone. The famous journalist, Herbert Swope said, "I cannot give you the formula for success, but I can give you the formula for failure—which is: Try to please everybody." Nothing will keep fear alive more than trying to be perfect or making everyone around you happy.

So, as fear grips you, unsheathe your dragon-slaying sword, inhale deeply, and symbolically slash your way past the doubt and strengthen your resolve. We are not born in fear. Fear is learned. We must unlearn it and replace it with focused awareness and courage.

The root of the word courage is *cour*, the French word for "heart." The idea that our emotions originate in our hearts goes back at least 2500 years and one of the earliest books to make this connection was called *On The Sacred Disease* about epilepsy written by followers of Hippocrates. At first in English in the 1300's, the word courage had meanings extending to all sorts of feelings one might attribute to one's heart: thoughts, feelings desires and passions—gentle, sexual, and violent. Over the centuries all those other meanings fell away.

Before French, courage came from Latin, and before that *cour* points back to an Indo-European *kerd,* meaning "heart." There is still enough similarity between this Indo-European *kerden* and the Old English *heorte* that you can see that the Indo-European root actually did percolate up into both Latin and Germanic languages. Therefore, writing from the heart is writing with courage; and if you approach your goals and dreams with courage, you will learn to act and write courageously, with heart.

When I have disappointments, fall short of my goals, or experience doubt and depression, I look at what I have written and remind myself, I took a chance. When fear is just about to overtake me, I remember that whether my script sells or everyone believes my writing stinks, I showed up and tried. I have developed sustainable motivation—no longer tied to naysayers—and you can too if you are willing to learn and commit to these suggested practices and attitudes. As I have, you will learn how to transform "I hope to," or "I would like to," into "I am a screenwriter," and "I will write a screenplay and reach the goals I've set."

Now, write the first few pages, or a "shitty" first draft. Make the time and show the courage to let fear go.

Works Cited

Card, Orson Scott. *How to Write Science Fiction & Fantasy*. Writers Digest Books, 2001.

de Becker, Gavin. *The Gift of Fear: And Other Survival Signals that Protect Us from Violence.* New York: Dell, 1998. Print.

Edison, Thomas. Quotation about Genius. *Harpers Monthly Magazine*, September 1932. (Note: The date of Edison's quote is debatable.)

Emig, Janet. "Writing as a Mode of Learning." *College Composition and Communication* 28.2 (1977): 122- 128. Print.

Hunt, Diana Scharf. *The Tao of Time*. New York: Simon & Schuster, 1991. Print.

Hunt, Diana Scharf, and Pam Hait. *Studying Smart*. New York: Harper, 1990.

Ikeda, Daisaku. *For Today and Tomorrow: Daily Encouragement.* World Press Tribune, 1999.

King, Stephen. *On Writing: A Memoir of the Craft*. New York: Pocket Books, 2001.

Lamott, Anne. *Bird by Bird: Some Instructions on Writing and Life*. New York: Anchor Books, 1995.

Oates, Joyce Carol. *The Faith of a Writer: Life, Craft, Art*. New York: HarperCollins, 2003.

Plimpton, George. "The Art of Fiction: Ernest Hemingway." *The Paris Review*, 5 (1958): 60-89.

White, Claire E. "A Conversation with Sue Grafton." *Writers Write: The Internet Writing Journal*. October 1999.

Sterling Anderson

Sterling Anderson is a three time NAACP Image Award nominee for best screenwriter and winner of the Movieguide Faith & Freedom Award and the Christopher Award. His movie *The Simple Life of Noah Dearborn* received an Emmy nomination for Dianne Wiest.

He has written for some of the most popular network television shows, such as *The Unit* on CBS, as well as NBC's *Medium* and *Heist*. His teleplay *The Simple Life of Noah Dearborn*, written for CBS starring Sidney Poitier, who won the NAACP Image Award for best actor. Sterling's extensive resume also includes screenplays written for Lions Gate, Disney, HBO, TriStar Pictures and Columbia Pictures.

A graduate in English from St. Mary's College, the accomplished writer also spent five years teaching screenwriting courses as an adjunct professor at the USC School of Cinematic Arts.

Born in Cincinnati, Ohio, Sterling spent his early childhood in Tuskegee, Alabama, before moving to Davis, California. His talents span far outside the world of writing. Sterling has a fifth degree black belt in Tae Kwon Do and was an award-winning winemaker in Napa Valley.

W. Douglas Baker

Doug is an award-winning teacher and Associate Professor at Eastern Michigan University, and is co-director of the Eastern Michigan Writing Project. He taught high school English for eleven years in central California, where he was particularly noted for mentoring young writers. He has written numerous articles for professional journals and books, has presented workshops and seminars in schools and at local, state and national conferences across the country, and has worked with thousands of high school and college students. Doug also holds a second degree black belt in Taekwondo.

Books By Sterling Anderson

Go To Script: Screenwriting Tips From A Pro

Five Seconds To Go

www.sterlingandersonwriter.com
www.sterlingwritersroom.com

Made in the USA
San Bernardino, CA
04 January 2019